KT-490-899

This Beautiful Land
BRITAIN

This Beautiful Land
BRITAIN

John Freeman and Sue Sharpe

BISON GROUP

First published in 1986 by
Bison Books Ltd.
Kimbolton House
117A Fulham Rd.
London SW3 6RL

Copyright © 1986 Bison Books Ltd

This revised and updated edition copyright
© 1992 Bison Books Ltd.

All rights reserved. No part of this
publication may be reproduced, stored in a
retrieval system or transmitted in any form
by any means, electronic, mechanical,
photocopying or otherwise, without first
obtaining the written permission of the
copyright owner.

ISBN 1-85841-012-6

Printed in China
Reprinted 1995

Acknowledgments

The publishers would like to thank the
following individuals and agencies for their
help in the preparation of this book:

Bronica UK Ltd
Katie Freeman
Luke Freeman
Studio Workshop Ltd
Martin Bristow, the designer

John Freeman supplied all the photographs
except for the following:

TPS/CLI: pages 21, 30-31, 68 (bottom), 72-73

Page 1: *The Cotswold village of Bursford,
Oxfordshire.*
Pages 2–3: *Ploughed fields in Oxfordshire.*
Pages 4–5: *Oil-seed rape field in Somerset.*

Contents

The Southwest

The wedge of land that forms the southwest of England contains some of the most striking countryside in southern England. The westerly county of Cornwall boasts England's longest coastline, indented with delightful bays and fishing villages; the moorland of Dartmoor, Devon, is bleak, rugged and beautiful; the elegant Georgian city of Bath retains its well-preserved Roman origins; while the port of Plymouth is steeped in naval history. With its pretty villages and country houses, it is little wonder that this region is highly popular with all manner of tourists, whose cars clog the narrow winding lanes in the summer.

Today, tourism is one of Cornwall's most important industries, and on a sunny day the fine beaches are crowded with holidaymakers, and the shops do a great trade in Cornish pasties, ice-cream and souvenirs. It is difficult to imagine that this was once the world's leading producer of copper and tin, having some 600 individual mines. A few mines still operate successfully, but most have long been abandoned, and their workings stand hidden and silent, the occasional remains of a brick chimney stack standing as a monument to a once prosperous industrial past. At Botallack on the north coast, just next to the stormy Atlantic, an old mine has been restored and shows clearly the conditions and hardships faced daily by its workers.

Like mining, fishing is a tough livelihood, where men pit their strength against the forces of nature. The fiord-like inlets form harbours, from which for centuries little fishing boats have braved the often violent seas. Standing on the most southerly tip at Land's End, or any other rugged headland, it is easy to imagine the dangers and anxieties faced by fishing communities as they struggled to extract a living. With the development of large factory ships, the fishing industry has gone into decline, as individuals can no longer compete. Some of these former fishermen have found it more profitable to turn their hand to tourism, and now use their craft to take aspiring fishermen out on sea-angling expeditions. A number of the pretty fishermen's cottages that line the narrow roads leading to harbours such as Mevagissey have been sold for holiday homes.

Previous pages: *Bedruthan Steps, Cornwall.*
Below: *The winding cobbled street of Goldhill, Shaftesbury, Dorset.*

Despite all these difficulties, the Cornish people are a tough and tenacious breed. Some Cornish people feel strongly that they ought to be totally independent from the rest of Britain. Contributing to this feeling is the way the River Tamar separates Cornwall from Devon, making it seem like an island. On the eastern side of the Tamar estuary lies Devonport, near Plymouth, one of the country's major naval dockyards where large grey warships are a familiar part of the landscape. This area has been important as a seaport and centre of naval activities for centuries; it was on Plymouth Hoe that Sir Francis Drake nonchalantly continued his historic game of bowls while the Spanish Armada drew closer.

No one can say for sure what would have happened if the Spanish had been successful, but any army invading England from this point almost certainly faced a long, bleak march across Dartmoor. This is mainly composed of swampy moorland bog and granite headlands, the highest of which is High Willhays, at 2039 feet. A daunting prospect for even today's well-shod walker, it was the obvious choice for a prison site in the mid-19th Century. Isolated by the rugged moor, it has been the secure home of some of Britain's most celebrated criminals.

Around Dartmoor are the richer pastures of Devon, famous for its clotted cream. Try it served with scones and jam, or strawberries in season. Like its neighbour, Somerset, Devon produces good, rich cheese; a fine way to spend a summer's day is to enjoy a ploughman's lunch of West Country Cheddar cheese washed down with a pint or two of 'scrumpy', the strong Somerset cider.

Perhaps scrumpy is partly responsible for the region's elaborate myths and legends. The area incorporating Devon, Somerset and Dorset, known as Wessex, was supposedly the Kingdom of King Arthur and his Knights of the Round Table. It is at Glastonbury Tor that Arthur is said to have received his Lady Guinevere from Melwas, and his grave is reputedly in Glastonbury Abbey.

While little concrete evidence exists to support the legends of King Arthur, Sir Lancelot and Merlin the Magician, the solid circle of Stonehenge stands testimony to ancient history. Still not completely understood, some people like to believe that invaders from space landed there, others that it is a place where the Druids worshipped the sun. Avebury, another stone circle, is equally impressive although less famous.

The Wessex countryside provided much of the inspiration for the novels of Thomas Hardy. Although many of the wilder areas such as his 'Egdon Heath' have become farmland, the towns still remain, like Dorchester, which is Casterbridge in his novel *The Mayor of Casterbridge*. A place made more recently familiar through its use in advertising is Goldhill Street in Shaftesbury. This steep, cobbled street, with its pleasant mixture of cob, brick and thatched cottages is more reminiscent of a

Left: *The view across the lake at Stourhead with the 16th-Century pantheon in the background.*

Above: *A carpet of bluebells heralds the summer in Black Dog Woods, Somerset.*
Left: *The shop-lined Pultney Bridge in Bath, Avon, was designed by Robert Adam.*
Right: *The remains of an early medieval castle at Launceston, the gateway to Cornwall.*

northern town than of the softer landscape of the south. The small market town of Frome, in Somerset, was an important woollen centre two centuries ago, and the old housing around its Trinity area looks like part of an 18th-Century Lancashire town.

One of the most memorable small towns on the south coast is Lyme Regis in Dorset. Once a thriving port, it retains an old-style atmosphere with its quaint old houses and steep, narrow streets. The 'Regis' dates from 1284 when it was granted a charter by Edward I, who used it as a base for his wars against the French. Its most notable historic contribution however was when the Duke of Monmouth landed there in 1685, declaring his intention to overthrow his uncle, James II. His attempt ended in failure at the Battle of Sedgemoor. Lyme Regis has achieved literary fame in providing the setting for John Fowles' novel *The French Lieutenant's Woman*, while the 14th-Century Cobb, the breakwater sheltering the attractive harbour, was the scene of Louisa's fall in Jane Austen's *Persuasion*.

The city of Bath combines history and beauty in a way that is hard to better. Its hot spring waters were discovered by the Romans, who created a spa town around them. The Roman Baths still remain as fascinating evidence of the sophistication of those times. The hot waters were channelled under floors and into pools to form an invigorating pleasure

Above: *The morning mist clears on Dartmoor, the wildest area in the southwest.*
Left: *The steep cobbled street at Clovelly, Devon, runs down to the harbour below.*
Below: *The wide expanse of sand and the rocky headland of Bedruthan Steps typify the north Cornish coast.*

dome where people would bathe in the healthy springs and discuss issues of the day. Watching the steam rising from the large pool today, it is amazing to think that this level of engineering was not equalled until the Industrial Revolution. It was about this time, in the 17th Century, that the city's beautiful Georgian crescents were built. The arc of Royal Crescent and the broad avenue of Pultney Street are two examples of this elegant splendour. Many of these buildings were designed by John Wood, who benefitted from having some wealthy and philanthropic sponsors. However, it was Beau Nash, a dandy, who made it fashionable to

travel all the way from London to take the waters in Bath.

Many of the little villages in Avon and Wiltshire such as Castle Combe, Corsham and Lacock (where Fox Talbot made the first photographic prints in 1838) still retain the image of the sleepy English village that some visitors to the country think typifies England as a whole. Enjoying a quiet drink in any of their hospitable pubs, it is hard to conceive of the urban sprawl of London that is no more than an hour's journey away.

Opposite: *A thatcher in a Somerset village prepares the straw to re-roof a cottage. In this part of the country, much of the straw is not baled but left in sheaves* (left) *solely for the purpose of thatching.*
Below: *The village of Lacock, Wiltshire, is entirely owned by the National Trust.*

The south-east of Britain is often referred to as the 'prosperous south' a label that can to some extent be justified by the fact that it includes the city of London. Not only is London England's capital in political terms but it is also the financial centre of the country, and the lure of opportunity and prosperity attracts people from far and wide. This is nothing new, and long before the legendary Dick Whittington, people came to London to seek their fortune, and still do so today.

Windsor Castle, in Berkshire, is probably the best-known castle in the world, being the favoured home of the Royal Family. William the Conqueror founded the present castle. The famous round tower dates from the 12th century. Henry I was the first monarch to use it as a royal residence. Like Buckingham Palace and St James's Palace in London, it is guarded by members of the Queen's Guards, whose red tunics and glossy black bearskin headdresses add a vivid splash of colour outside the white-grey stone walls.

Previous pages: *The quay at Bosham West Sussex, lined with cottages, many with raised doorways to protect them from the water.*
Right: *The carriageway leading through the Great Park to Windsor Castle.*
Left: *With the approach of autumn, leaves begin to fall from the trees at Devil's Punchbowl, Surrey.*
Below: *A rose-covered thatched cottage in Lasham, Hampshire.*

Above: *The vast expanse of the North Downs, seen here at Wrotham, Kent, stretches all the way from Surrey to the Channel ports of Dover and Folkestone.*
Right: *Oast houses in Kent were originally designed to dry hops, used to make beer, but* most have now been converted to luxury country homes.
Below: *Canterbury, whose history predates Roman times, has many historic buildings that have survived civil war and, more recently, the Blitz in World War II.*

In sudden contrast to this somewhat sur-burban country landscape is an area of rugged heathland and forest at Hindhead, near Hasle-mere. Here a vast cauldron has been carved out of the ground by the forces of erosion, and is known as the Devil's Punchbowl. Walking through the woods to the edge of this great basin one is rewarded with a panoramic view over heather and gorse towards Guildford. Strangely enough, another large chasm on the South Downs near Brighton bears a very similar name. Devil's Dyke is a huge Vee-shaped cleft in the downs giving extensive views over the weald. Legend has it that the Devil was upset at the growth of Christian settlements in Sussex and began to dig a trench towards the sea which would flood the weald and destroy the churches. However, the noise of his labours disturbed a woman, who held up a candle to see what was going on. Frightened by the light, which he took to be the rising sun, the Devil fled, leaving his work unfinished.

The advent of the railways in the 18th Century not only affected travel to and from London, but also gave access to coastal resorts in the south, to where the city's rich and fashionable folk would travel to bathe in the sea. Brighton, which is perhaps the best-known of these resorts, owes much of its architectural heritage to the period. Many of its crescents, squares and terraces are of the same design as those in London's Regent's Park and Belgravia. John Nash, the designer of Regent's Park as well as many of London's famous buildings, was commissioned by George III's son, the Prince of Wales, to redesign the Royal Pavilion in Brighton. The result caused some controversy, its somewhat exotic design being described by William Cobbett as 'a square box, a large Norfolk turnip and four onions'. Yet it still stands and its eccentric façade has become a feature of Brighton. Its lush interiors make it a fascinating place to visit.

Most resorts on the south coast boast a pier. These architectural gems of an earlier age rest on spindly legs and extend into the sea. Piers are places for strolling, sitting in the cool sea breeze, fishing and for summer entertainment such as plays and musical revues. Sadly, many

Right: *Early morning mist shrouds Bodiam, in East Sussex, one of the best-preserved medieval castles.*
Below: *The West Gate of the old city walls towers over the River Stour at Canterbury, Kent.*

Left: *Mermaid Street is one of many picturesque streets in Rye, East Sussex. Rye is one of the original Cinque Ports, established to defend the coast from possible invasion by the French in the 11th Century.*
Below: *One of Rochester's many attractive historic buildings.*

piers have fallen into disrepair and have become dangerous, such as Brighton's West Pier. Its sister, the Palace Pier, however, is as popular as ever, and even more gaudy. Holiday-makers and tourists alike stroll along the pier to enjoy the fresh sea air.

A familiar profile on the south-east shoreline that must be mentioned is that of the famous white cliffs of Dover. The sight of these looming up in the distance is always impressive to those arriving by sea for the first time, but for those returning to England after a long absence, it is when they truly know they are home again!

Above: *A view of the Tower of London and Traitor's Gate, on the Thames.*
Left: *Speakers' Corner, Hyde Park.*
Right: *A soldier of the Scot's Guard on duty outside St James's Palace, London.*
Below: *The bright neon lights of London's West End.*

Wales

*C*roeso i Gymru – 'Welcome to Wales'. With so many languages and dialects disappearing it is very refreshing to find the Welsh language flourishing. In such a small country it says much for the spirit of its people that many of the Welsh traditions are kept strongly alive.

In Caernarfon, in North Wales, Welsh is the most commonly spoken language, and visitors may be forgiven for thinking they are in a place far from Britain. Caernarfon town nestles within the old town walls, beneath the ramparts of Caernarfon Castle. This was built by Edward I in the 13th Century, like many other castles in North Wales, and it towers impressively over the Menai Strait. Edward's son was born here in 1284, and in 1301 he offered him to the Welsh people as 'Prince of Wales'. Since that time it has been traditional for the reigning English monarch to present his or her eldest son to Wales. This investiture ceremony was last performed at Caernarfon Castle in 1969 with Prince Charles.

Previous pages: *Horseshoe Pass, near Llangollen, is typical of the landscape in the north-eastern part of Wales.*
Right: *Caernarfon Castle stands on the Menai Strait; Prince Charles was invested here as Prince of Wales in 1969.*
Below: *The daunting heights of Llanberis Pass, Snowdonia, present a challenge taken up by many enthusiastic rock climbers.*

A few miles inland from Caernarfon is Snowdonia, a vast area of lakes and mountains with small villages hidden in wooded valleys. It is one of the most beautiful parts of Wales. It is dominated by the lofty heights of Snowdon, which at 3560 feet is the highest mountain in Wales. Climbing this peak presents a challenge taken up by many people, but it need not be an arduous ascent, because there are a number of routes of varying difficulty. However, as with walking or climbing in any exposed area, conditions can suddenly become dangerous when the mists descend and precautions should always be taken. The view from Snowdon's summit on a clear day is worth all the effort. It is one of the most extensive sights in the whole country; on a good day even the Wicklow Mountains in Ireland can be seen. Those not in shape to climb have the easy alternative of ascending in Britain's only mountain railway, first opened in 1896. The steam engine pulling the carriage puffs and pants its way from Llanberis up nearly five miles of track to the summit, making frequent stops for water. The railway, and other narrow-gauge tracks that run through some of Wales's finest scenery, rivals Snowdon in popularity. They originated in the late 18th Century, when increasing demand for slate mined in the area made quarry owners consider more efficient means of transportation than packhorses. In 1801 Richard Pennant, owner of the Penrhyn Quarry at Bethesda, was the first to build a

narrow-gauge railway for this purpose. It ran from Bethesda to Port Penrhyn at Bangor to a gauge of two feet. In 1836 the Ffestiniog Railway opened, worked by gravity, which also had a two-foot gauge. Many other new lines were opened, some of which were horse drawn. In 1863 the Ffestiniog Railway was the first to adopt steam traction on this type of gauge, and

Left: *A view of some of the colourful buildings in the famous Italianate village of Portmeirion, designed by Sir Clough Williams-Ellis.*
Below: *Trees come down to the shoreline of Lake Vyrnwy, a reservoir in mid-Wales.*

introduced passenger trains two years later. Although these railways expanded in the 19th Century with the growth of tourism, the decline in the slate industry in the later part of the century and the increasing flexibility of road transport at the beginning of the next caused many closures. It is the preservation movement who are to be thanked for the reopening of several of these lines for tourist traffic, as at Ffestiniog, Talyllyn, Welshpool and Llanfair.

North Wales is full of pretty valleys, lakes and streams. At Beddgelert, south of Snowdon, the river tumbles over rocks and under bridges,

its banks filled with glorious purple rhododendron flowers during the early summer months. To the south of Beddgelert is Porthmadoc, on Tremadog Bay, where the 17th-Century-style Italianate village of Portmeirion is tucked away on a wooded peninsula. This fascinating complex of buildings was designed in 1926 by the Welsh architect Sir Clough Williams-Ellis, a long-standing campaigner against the destruction of the British countryside by unsightly development. He was determined to prove that an old site could be enhanced through development rather than the reverse, and the result is a pleasing, colourful inter-

mingling of styles. Loosely modelled on the Italian fishing village of Portofino, it incorporates restored 18th-Century English cottages and a 19th-Century house on the waterfront made into a hotel. Visitors entering by the bridge house are confronted by Mediterranean pastel-painted buildings, pools and fountains and shrubs and flowers. The architect's success in his aim is reflected in its popularity. A number of famous writers have

Above: *At the end of the season, lobster pots line the quay at Barmouth, on the Welsh coast. Traditional fishing methods still provide an income for some Welsh families.*
Right: *Constitution Hill presents a lofty background to the elegant crescent of houses looking out to Aberystwyth Bay.*
Below: *The amber light of the setting sun highlights the unusually weathered rocks at Dunraven Bay, South Wales.*

stayed here, such as George Bernard Shaw, H G Wells, John Steinbeck and Noel Coward, who wrote *Blythe Spirit* here.

Although not quite so startling as Portmeirion, there are many interesting villages and towns along the coast of Wales and around Cardigan Bay. One of the largest resorts is Aberystwyth, the home of the University of Wales and the National Library of Wales. The original college was a splendid Gothic Building on the seafront by the pier, but it was soon outgrown and a new college was built on Penglais Hill. From the top of Constitution Hill there is a spectacular view south.

In the south-west of Wales stands Pembroke Castle. Although damaged by guns in 1648

Left: *One of the steam engines operating on the narrow-gauge railway at Ffestiniog takes on fresh water.*
Below: *Beddgelert, on the River Nantgwynant, is a well-known beauty spot.*

during the Civil War, it remains one of the best-preserved Norman Castles in Britain. Across the water of Milford Haven is the far less attractive site of Britain's largest oil refineries. Although it has brought much-needed employment to the region, it has spoilt this beautiful part of Dyfed. The main industrial centres of Wales, such as Swansea and Port Talbot, are along the southern coast. Here vast steel mills are set against a background of mountains. Further east, the city of Cardiff has a more civic atmosphere because of its status, since 1955, as the Welsh Capital. North and South Wales are not only different in their landscape but also in their working history. The rise and fall of the coal and steel industry in the southern valleys has left scars not only on the countryside but also on the people, who have struggled to survive through economic depressions and pit disasters. Many people regard Wales as mountainous and this image is quickly confirmed by travelling north from

Cardiff into the Black Mountains and the Brecon Beacons. Although rugged and sometimes bleak, their beauty must have brought some relief to the people who have laboured in the mines or iron industries since the 18th and 19th Centuries.

Singing has been so important in Wales's heritage that it would be difficult to think of the country without it. The Eisteddfod, a festival of song and dance, has become a world-renowned event. There are two main eisteddfods, the Llangollen and the National, the latter being held alternatively in North and South Wales. In addition to these large events there are countless male voice choirs, many of which have their origins in the mines.

The visitor to Wales is continually taken by surprise. This small country offers an infinite variety of different landscapes and coastal regions and a multitude of ancient and historical sites and buildings. The spirit of the Welsh is alive throughout the principality.

Most regions of Britain contain a variety of landscapes, but surely none can rival the dramatic contrasts of the Midlands. Gentle and well-tended farmland rises into the bleak and sometimes dangerous contours of the Peak District. Small villages and hamlets of Cotswold stone, where life seems to pass with a timeless quality of conservatism, stand within a few miles of the huge sprawling conurbations of the West Midlands, where industry has irreparably ravaged the countryside. The unrest of the inner city areas seems far away in time and space from nearby rural areas which provided the inspiration for some of Britain's greatest writers and composers.

England's greatest poet and playwright, William Shakespeare, was born in Henley Street, Stratford-on-Avon, in 1564. His fame is such that this Warwickshire town is second only to London in the amount of visitors it receives every year. They arrive in droves, not only to visit the house of his birth, but also the cottage of his wife, Anne Hathaway, whom he

Previous pages: The River Wye, seen from Symond's Yat, winds its way through the countryside to the town of Hereford.
Right: Warwick Castle seen reflected in the water of the River Avon, which acts as part of its protective moat.
Below: This cottage in Stratford-on-Avon, Warwickshire, is the birthplace of William Shakespeare's wife, Anne Hathaway.

married in 1582. Her fine, timber-framed house is the epitome of an old English country home, and although damaged by fire in 1969, it has been lovingly restored. In 1597 Shakespeare bought New Place, on the corner of Chapel Street and Chapel Lane, where he died in 1616. The house no longer exists but its foundations are in the garden of Thomas Nash, who married Shakespeare's granddaughter. Nash's house is now a museum. Shakespeare is buried in the grounds of Holy Trinity Church and his gravestone bears the inscription:

Good frend for Jesus sake forbeare
To digg the dust enclosed heare
Bleste be ye man yt spares thes stones
And curst be he yt moves my bones.

Oxford is synonymous with its university, founded in the 12th Century by Henry II. When unrest in Oxford in 1209 forced the university to close for a time, some of its students moved east to a small town called Cambridge, where they formed a new university. Oxford and Cambridge, known collectively as Oxbridge, are the country's foremost universities and have achieved a worldwide academic reputation. Most of Oxford's colleges cluster around the High Street, and from above this area looks like a well-preserved medieval city. It attracts many visitors, who come to wander round the college quadrangles and admire the fine architecture.

Above: *Christ Church College, Oxford, from across the War Memorial Gardens.*

It is not only for its university that Oxford has achieved fame, however, but also for its motor cars. William Morris (later viscount Nuffield) created the forerunner to British Leyland by manufacturing cars with the name Morris Oxford. These cars were to revolutionize motor transport in Britain, and in 1920 the Morris Cowley overtook the Model T Ford as Britain's biggest selling car. Morris also adopted other local names for his cars such as

Isis – from Themesis, the Roman name for the River Thames, which runs through the city. Locally the river is known as the Isis, but exactly where this starts and ends is unclear. As well as providing the area with industry and employment, Morris also endowed Oxford with one of its newest colleges, Nuffield College.

A feature that extends throughout the Midlands is the network of canals. These can be traced back to Roman times, but really proliferated in the late 16th Century. The Grand Union, Shropshire, Oxford and Coven-

try Canals are just some that increased the ease with which goods could be carried, and therefore increased the prosperity of the region. Today many are being restored but most of the traffic sailing on them are pleasure craft.

A common image of this region is portrayed by the industrial Midlands, at the heart of which are cities like Coventry, Birmingham and Wolverhampton, which merge into a vast untidy mass of concrete tower blocks and smoking factories. In Arnold Bennett's novels, set around the Staffordshire potteries district, he creates a certain romanticism in the midst of working people's struggles to survive and cope with the innovations and progress of industry. But nowadays there seems little romance about this area as industry declines and work is scarce.

It is a welcome relief to arrive at the foothills of the Derbyshire Peak District. The small towns nestling here have their own unique

Below: *The Cotswold-stone cottages of Lower Slaughter, Gloucestershire, stand next to the River Eye.*

histories and associations. For example, George Eliot set her novel *Adam Bede* in Wirksworth, and D H Lawrence lived near Middleton for a while. Bakewell is renowned for its Bakewell Tarts, and Matlock Bath has been a well-visited spa town for several centuries.

Eyam is over 100 miles from London, yet it had the misfortune to contract the Plague in the 17th Century. It began when a box of contaminated clothes was sent to a tailor; his family soon became infected and died. The disease rapidly spread through the area and by the time it subsided the local population of

around 350 had been reduced to about 100. One activity that these towns and villages have in common is their adherence to the pagan ritual of well-dressing. This involves decorating wells during the summer months with highly elaborate and colourful designs made up of flower petals.

The highest and wildest part of this region is the north, where the loftiest peak is Kinder Scout, 2088 feet, which is bordered by the Snake Pass in the east and Rush-up Edge to the south. In the early 1930s the rambling associations organized a 'mass trespass' on Kinder

Scout to protest about being denied access to the moorland. About a thousand people took part. They were met by keepers and scuffles broke out. Although the land is still privately owned, attitudes have changed and hiking is permitted. The Pennine Way begins near here, the 250-mile long walk to the Borders Region.

The country around this area is wild and remote, with breath-taking views over strangely shaped rock formations which can look ghostly and sinister when the mist comes down. At these times it becomes a hostile and dangerous area where it is only too easy to get lost or have an accident. On a fine day however, the view from the top is worth the effort.

Opposite: *Little Moreton Hall, Cheshire, is one of the best surviving Elizabethan buildings in the country.*
Left: *Intricately patterned drystone walls typify Derbyshire.*
Below: *A disused railway viaduct stands over the River Wye at Monsal Dale.*

Previous pages: *Ludham on the Norfolk Broads provides a mooring place for many boats.*
Right: *The quadrangle of St John's College Cambridge, and* (opposite) *the Bridge of Sighs that crosses the River Cam.*
Below right: *The organ in the beautiful chapel of King's College.*

*E*ast Anglia has not been endowed with a very exciting image. It is most characteristically thought of as flat and featureless, modern farming methods having removed many of the hedgerows and trees. But although there are parts which have suffered this fate, with sometimes disastrous ecological consequences, the area is far more than a vast prairie. Within its boundaries lie forests, waterways and a coastline which provides a haven for many varieties of wildlife. Historic buildings include the Queen's summer residence at Sandringham and the famous university city of Cambridge.

Cambridge is a very appropriate place from which to survey this region, as East Anglia fans out eastwards from this point. Important as a centre of learning since the 13th Century, it could be said that Cambridge consists essentially of its university. Although the oldest of its 31 colleges is Peterhouse, endowed in 1284 by Hugh de Balsham, Bishop of Ely, it is probably King's College that attracts the most visitors. The famous chapel, seen from across the River Cam, draws admiration for its fine Gothic architecture, but the real pleasure lies inside. Here, the prismatic effects of the sunlight filtering gently through the 16th-Century stained glass windows bestows an airy tranquility and beauty, but for inspiration nothing can beat the King's College choir in full voice.

In Thaxted, Essex, one timber-framed building, Cutler's Castle, dominates the High Street. Built by the Cutler's Guild when Thaxted was the centre of Britain's cutlery trade, it was used as a meeting house. From the Castle, a cobbled street which winds up the hill to the church is lined on one side with similar timber-framed houses. One of these bears the name 'Dick Turpin's Cottage', suggesting it was once the home of this legendary highwayman. It is exploring country lanes to discover such villages and hamlets that still retain the essence of bygone days that provides the real pleasures of the counties Essex, Suffolk and Norfolk.

Although the East Anglian landscape lacks the impact of lakes, mountains or rolling hills, it has a surprising wealth of flora and fauna. Wicken Fen, north of Cambridge, is the protected home of numerous birds, animals and plant life. Off the Essex coast lies Foulness Island and Maplin Sands, once the proposed site of London's third airport. Its extensive sandflats and saltings have a haunting, desolate atmosphere. It is a favourite place for ornithologists. Many varieties of waders, such as the oystercatcher, knot, dunlin and curlew, gather there to feed on the small creatures inhabiting the vast sandy area.

Epping Forest has been owned and administered by the Corporation of London since 1878, and since the turn of the century has been an

extremely popular place every Easter, Whitsun and August bank holiday. Owing to increased mobility, every sunny weekend it is now full of visitors, who walk, have picnics, play games or just lie in the sun. Its 6000 acres of hornbeam, birch and beech trees stretch from Walthamstow to Epping and, despite the roads that cross it, it is still very easy to get lost in its numerous leafy glades.

Above: *Minsmere Nature Reserve, near Dunwich in Suffolk.*
Left: *The River Ouse flows through Godmanchester in Cambridgeshire.*
Below: *Brancaster Bay, on the Norfolk coast.*

The River Stour in Flatford runs through Dedham Vale, in the northern part of Essex. This area is immortalized in the paintings of

John Constable, and is generally known as 'Constable Country'. In pictures such as *The Haywain* he, possibly more than any other artist of his time, captured the essence of the English countryside.

Suffolk is a county that has quietly achieved popularity. Both its country villages and coastal resorts, such as Southwold, Walbers-

Left: *The windmill seen beyond these almshouses in Thaxted, Essex, is a museum. Two examples of timber-framed buildings in this region are Dick Turpin's Cottage in Thaxted* (below left) *and the Moot Hall, Aldeburgh, Suffolk.*

wick and Aldeburgh, are filled with visitors in the summer months, lying on the sandy beaches and enjoying the hospitality of their old-style pubs. One stretch of beach however, called Shingle Street, is less accommodating. As its name implies, it is a long strip of shingle, and the only sounds which accompany the intrepid walker are the crunch of shingle underfoot, the roar of the north wind and the shrill cry of the seagulls. Desolate as it is, it has a stark beauty that can only be realized on foot. Walking is the best way to appreciate many other parts of this area, like Tunstall Forest, Cove-hithe and Dunwich Common, which is part of the Minsmere Nature Reserve.

Much of East Anglia's coast is under constant threat of erosion by the sea; Dunwich is a dramatic victim of this. Over the last 400 years the sea has advanced inland about a quarter of a mile. Once a prosperous and busy town, Dunwich today is a small village, having lost a large number of its buildings to the sea.

East of Norwich, the capital of East Anglia, lie the Norfolk Broads. These shallow, reed-fringed lakes are linked together by a series of streams, rivers and dykes, forming about 200 miles of navigable waterway. Negotiating a boat down the Norfolk Broads is a popular holiday attraction, and one which contributes to the region's economy. The high reeds often

obscure the water channels from view, resulting in the rather bizarre sight of a set of sails appearing to cross fields, which can understandably confuse the passing walker or motorist.

Whatever the popular image of East Anglia, it is the chosen retreat of the Royal Family, whose 7000-acre estate at Sandringham lies west of Norwich, near the Wash. Its country park, open to the public, is famous for its rhododendrons, which in full bloom provide vivid colour to a forest of cedar, birch and pine trees. East Anglia is certainly not an area to be overlooked; its pleasures have to be gently explored and savoured.

Ulster

Northern Ireland is like another English county. Despite being across the Irish Sea, it has more in common with a rural English landscape or the Scottish Highlands than the adjoining provinces of the Irish Republic. This is not surprising since the northern coast is only separated from Scotland by a narrow ribbon of water, and the Ulster hills were a continuation of the Highlands and Uplands. Five of Northern Ireland's six counties meet at Lough Neagh, a vast lake formed in the collapsed centre of a mass of volcanic lava. It is this volcanic rock, also found in the Inner Hebrides, the Faeroe Islands and Iceland, which make up some of the region's most distinctive landmarks, such as the Giant's Causeway, the cliffs of Antrim, and Cavehill, overlooking Belfast.

The region is made up from six of the nine counties that originally formed the province of Ulster, which were combined as Northern Ireland in 1922, and granted partial self-government under the British crown. Irish history has been a continuous story of invasion,

Previous pages: *View towards Enniskillen, County Fermanagh, over Lough MacNean.*
Opposite: *Carrickfergus harbour and castle, County Antrim.*
Left: *The Mountains of Mourne rise up from the sea in County Down.*
Below: *The remains of Dunluce Castle, County Antrim, stand perilously on the cliff edge.*

land seizure and battles for religious freedom, but while Partition resolved this situation for the Irish Republic, Northern Ireland lives with a permanently high level of religious animosity and conflict.

The central and southern parts of Ireland were always more favoured by foreign invaders, who found them more accessible and accommodating than the rugged west and northwest. The early Vikings were followed in the 11th Century by the Anglo-Normans, who arrived from England and took over the government of the country, based around Dublin and the east coast. It was really not until the 16th Century that Elizabeth I, fearing a Spanish attack through Ireland, sent military forces to Ulster. Despite much resistance from Irish Catholics, the country became dominated by the superior strength of Protestant England. To consolidate their position, the English government drove the native population off their lands and replaced them with loyal Protestant settlers. England's James I sent many thousands of Scots and English as part of this 'plantation', and further efforts were made to spread Anglicanism and suppress Catholicism.

The city of Derry became known as Londonderry in the early 17th Century when it was

Left: *Giant's Causeway, County Antrim.*
Below: *Whiskey stills inside Bushmills Distillery, County Antrim.*

granted to the City of London as part of the scheme of the New Plantation of Ulster. Under an agreement with James II, the Citizens of London undertook the plantation of large areas of forfeited land which then formed the county of Coleraine. To defend Londonderry – or Derry as it is still generally known – the England-based Irish Society built the impressive city walls, which still remain today. These were to withstand several sieges, the most memorable being in 1688, when Derry supported William of Orange against Catholic James II. This event is commemorated in a finely detailed stained-glass window in the city's Guildhall.

The coast line round the county of Antrim in the north and east contains some of the most striking and beautiful scenery in Northern Ireland. In the northwest, the white chalk cliffs are speckled with caves, and high on the cliff above Castlerock stands the Italian-inspired Mussenden Temple, and the ruins of Downhill Castle, both built by the Earl-Bishop of Bristol and Derry, probably the most extravagant bishop who ever lived. An obsessive collector, he hunted Europe for works of art to put in his palace, which housed the finest private collection in Ireland. He also liked to hold parties at his palace, and at one of these, he organized a horse race over Magilligan Strand for clergymen of different denominations, in which the Presbyterians won against their Anglican competitors.

Left: *The grand 18th-Century façade of Florence Court, County Fermanagh.*
Below: *Open country near Newry, County Armagh.*

In some places the edge of the sea is chequered with white boulders and black basalts, formed from volcanic lava. The most spectacular volcanic formation is the famous Giant's Causeway, which consists of about 37,000 regular hexagonal-shaped basalt columns, packed closely together at different heights. They form a honeycomb of stepping stones which descend from the base of the cliff and vanish into the sea. Formed 60,000,000 years ago by the cooling and shrinking of molten lava, some clusters of columns make distinctive shapes which have been given appropriate names, such as Giant's Organ, the Punchbowl and the Wishing Chair. As a natural wonder it is very striking, whether dark and brooding in a thunderstorm, or lit by the golden rays of the setting sun.

Not far away from this landmark is the home of another traditional association with Ireland. Bushmills Distillery is the world's oldest whiskey distillery, and although it was granted its official Licence to Distil in 1608, the Irish *usquebaugh* (water of life) was drunk centuries before this time. As long ago as 1276, a Norman captain, Sir Robert Savage, campaigning in

North Antrim, is said to have given each of his soldiers a 'mighty draught of *usquebaugh*' before battle.

As well as whiskey, another industry that is associated with Ireland is linen. This developed significantly after the 17th Century through the activities of Huguenot refugees who sought sanctuary in Ulster. By the 19th Century the central area, especially mid-Antrim, around Ballymena, contained numerous water-powered mills, dyeworks, bleachworks, weaving factories and beetling mills.

It was the famous Battle of the Boyne, where James II was beaten by William, that sealed the Protestant victory in Ireland and left Catholics politically helpless, a state further exacerbated by the enactment of a series of anti-Catholic measures called the Penal Laws. It was not for several centuries that the situation was to change radically, through campaigns for Catholic Emancipation, and in the 19th Century through the movements for national independence, land reform, and a constitutional movement for Home Rule and a separate Irish parliament. This was not to be implemented until after World War I; the Anglo-Irish Treaty was signed in 1921 and ratified a year later. This separated Northern Ireland from the rest of the country, which

Left: *The impressive drive leading to Stormont, near Belfast.*
Below: *Killary Harbour, County Galway.*

Above: *Even this shed door reflects the vibrant colour of Ireland.*
Left: *Mussenden Temple, built on the edge of the cliff at Downhill, County Derry.*

was made the Irish Free State. Northern Ireland was governed by a regional parliament based in Stormont, near Belfast. In the 1970s, political unrest forced the suspension of Stormont, which was replaced by direct rule from Westminster.

The nine glens of Antrim cut down to the coast in the east, forming lovely wooded valleys ending in pretty coastal villages. The central part of Northern Ireland is quite flat and rural, but this is broken by the broad range of Sperrin Mountains, which turn purple-brown with heather in late summer. In the south-east, the famous Mountains of Mourne dominate the coastline, their 15 peaks rising majestically up from the sea, while in the south-west, the lakes of County Fermanagh present a more tranquil aspect. The 50-mile stretch of Upper and Lower Lough Erne is separated in the middle by the county town of Enniskillen. The water is studded with little islands, some of which contain fascinating religious remains, such as the double-faced

Janus pagan figure on Boa Island. The origins of this and other figures are still the subject of controversy.

Belfast was only a village in the 17th Century but with the growth of industries like linen, cotton, ropemaking, engineering and tobacco it soon blossomed into a major port and achieved city status in the 1880s. For over a century its shipyards have held a worldwide reputation. While Belfast is the industrial and administrative capital of Northern Ireland, the ancient city of Armagh is its ecclesiastical capital. It has two cathedrals, one Roman Catholic and the other Anglican, both called St Patrick's, which face each other on different hills.

This opposition of Protestant and Catholic is reflected in the continuing religious tension and conflict. The beauty of Northern Ireland's mountains, lakes and glens, and its well-farmed countryside may be reminiscent of parts of England and Scotland, but the uncomfortable presence of the British Army, with their road blocks and armoured cars, and the fenced off police stations in towns and cities, lend a different atmosphere, and serve as reminders that peace and beauty do not necessarily coincide.

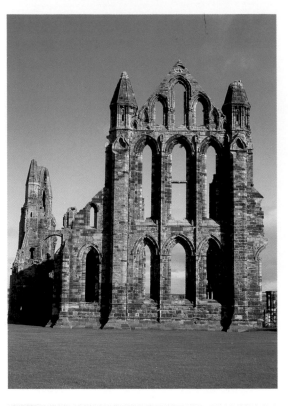

There is a sense of hardness about Northern England. Certainly not hard in an unfriendly way, as some Southerners are inclined to think, nor in its architecture, nor the relative lack of lush green pastures, but in the toughness and resilience that it has taken, and in some places still takes, to survive. Many novels set in this part of the country reflect this, such as the Brontës' novels in the 19th Century and life in the Depression as portrayed in Greenwood's *Love on the Dole*. It is in the more remote parts that people still lead a rugged existence, battling against the elements. During the cold winter months, howling winds over the moors hurl needle-sharp raindrops against the skin, and livestock may be lost in the storms and snow. There is no piped gas to isolated farms and houses and

Previous pages: *Looking towards Windermere from the summit of Langdale Pikes, Lake District.*
Left: *The gaunt ruins of Whitby Abbey, Yorkshire, stand high above the sea.*
Below: *An areal view of Thirlmere Lake, in the Lake District, seen in winter.*

sometimes no electricity, and reliance is placed on traditional fuels like wood and coal. Grim as this picture may sound, even in winter the countryside has a dramatic appeal and in the summer sun it is fresh and beautiful.

High on the moors behind Haworth in Yorkshire stands the foreboding ruin of High Witham, said to be the 'Wuthering Heights' of Emily Brontë's vivid novel. Wandering across these bleak, wind-swept hills, it is easy to evoke the atmosphere of those times, when the Brontë family was dogged by illness and tragedy, and the three sisters would try to escape from reality by writing stories and taking long walks over the moors. Today the parsonage where they lived and died has been opened to the public, and is very popular with visitors. Although some rooms re-create how it used to be, it is perhaps the graveyard in front that is most poignant. Its closely clustered gravestones are covered in green lichen and goats graze on what little grass remains. A cobbled street leads down into the village and to the Black Bull Inn where Branwell Brontë drank himself into an early grave. Up on the

moors, the waterfall where supposedly Charlotte caught the chill that was to end in her death in 1855 has been named after the family.

Only a few miles over this moor lies the town of Keighley, which a century ago epitomized the new prosperity brought by industrialization. Although local mill owners flourished it had harsh effects on the living and working conditions of local inhabitants. Today some of the woollen mills still operate but their profitability has declined in the face of competition, mainly from the Far East.

The landscape east from Keighley becomes flatter and less rugged as industrial towns give way to farming villages. As one approaches York, the twin towers of the Minster come into view, high above all other buildings. York Minster is a massive structure, 524 feet long and 249 feet wide across its transepts. It has been a religious site since Saxon times, but the present building was begun in the 13th Century. Some of its lovely stained glass win-

Below: *A rowan tree in full colour at Grange, in Borrowdale, Lake District.*

dows date from the 12th Century. In the mid-1960s serious structural faults were discovered, necessitating a large-scale repair programme; this suffered a setback in 1984 when the Minster was damaged by fire. York is an attractive walled city on the River Ouse, and many of its old streets, such as Stonegate and The Shambles, are so tightly packed with medieval buildings that they almost seem to be trying to push each other out of the way.

The bustle of the university city of York soon recedes and moving northwards towards the coast, green farmland disappears into the North Yorkshire moors. This vast area was once forested, but over thousands of years the trees have been cut down by the inhabitants of various settlements. Without this cover, the topsoil was eroded so much that only the hardiest of plants could survive, such as heather. In late summer this undulating moorland becomes a carpet of purple, speckled with grey rocks and white, grazing sheep.

It is through this moorland scenery that one reaches the fishing town of Whitby. The narrow winding streets, full of pantiled houses

and shops, all seem to lead down to the quay. Brightly coloured fishing boats jostle together for mooring space in the harbour. A familiar sight is the dredging boat, *The Esk*, named after the river that bisects the town, delving into the water in its daily battle against an onslaught of silt washed in by the North Sea. High on the west cliff overlooking the harbour stands a statue of James Cook, the famous sea captain who made his epic voyages around the world in ships that were built in Whitby.

On the opposite clifftop, above the older part of town, stand the brooding ruins of Whitby Abbey, reached by a steep flight of stone steps from Church Street. From here it is possible to take a lovely, albeit bracing, walk along the cliff path to Robin Hood's Bay. On a cold, foggy night, with the haunting sound of the fog siren, the atmosphere feels almost sinister, which is probably why Bram Stoker chose it as the setting for his famous nove; *Dracula*, written in 1897.

The impressive length of Hadrian's Wall can be traced all the way from Newcastle in the east to Carlisle in the west. It seems somewhat strange that such a wall was required at all in

some areas, as the terrain itself should have been enough to deter even the most determined attempts to traverse it.

It was the countryside south of here, in Cumbria, that was to inspire the poet William Wordsworth in the 19th Century, when he lived in Dove Cottage, near Grasmere. The Lake District is a compact area of great beauty, with view upon view of lakes and mountains. In Wordsworth's day, it was perhaps easier to 'wander lonely as a cloud', as his famous poem 'The Daffodils' suggests, but today, especially in the summer, the area is rather crowded. The region has become extremely popular with tourists, and on fine days the lower slopes are covered with strolling figures. The more serious walker however can still find unpopulated areas by climbing high above the lakes at Langdale Pikes for instance, or by exploring the rugged heights of Wasdale. The Lake District is a lovely place in every season, and the colour changes are as dramatic as the landscape itself. The greens and blues of summer blend into autumn russet and gold, followed by the brilliant white of snow-capped peaks with maroon-coloured hillsides in winter. Spring miraculously brings fresh green foliage and flowers.

Left: *Bamburgh Castle, Northumberland.*
Right: *The Parsonage, Haworth, West Yorkshire, was the home of the famous Brontë family.*
Below: *The River Tweed, which at its eastern end divides England from Scotland.*

Scotland

*B*ritain is not a large country, and the distance from the southern coast to the northern islands is comparatively short, yet for many people, including the English, Scotland is an unknown land. For some it is merely a caricature of kilts and tartans, haggis and whisky and poems by Robbie Burns delivered in a strong Scottish accent, all in a setting of mountains, lakes and purple heather. They remain unaware of the nature of its history, culture and people.

The England-Scotland border is formed in the east by the River Tweed. A common sight are fishermen standing thigh-deep in waders

Previous pages: *Tulloch village, near Loch Laggan in the Scottish Highlands.*
Above: *Edinburgh Castle is unusual in being built on a hill rather than by water, unlike moated Caerlaverock Castle* (below), *near the Solway Firth.*
Right: *Melrose Abbey in the Border.*

Right: *The misty mountains of Glencoe in the Highland region of Scotland.*
Below: *Looking over Scapa Flow from Mainland, the largest of the Orkney Islands.*

trying to catch the prized river trout. Where the Tweed is joined by the Teviot stands the beautiful town of Kelso. Here the majority of streets are still cobbled. The well-preserved buildings are decorated with window boxes.

Probably one of the best ways to gain an introduction to Scotland is to drive through Border country to Edinburgh, Scotland's capital city since 143. In contrast to most other cities in Britain, Edinburgh was built on hills rather than on rivers or estuaries. Its famous castle dominates the centre and sits high on a rocky mound rather like the topping of a large cake. Instead of enticing the on-looker, however, it rather exudes an air of impenetrability. Today it is open for the visitor to explore, and wonderful views of the city and the surrounding countryside can be enjoyed from its battle-

ments. The annual arts festival also draws many people, and has gained a worldwide reputation for its avant-garde plays, films and revues.

As one crosses the Firth of Forth by car one sees the rail bridge made famous in Alfred Hitchcock's film *The 39 Steps*. The countryside becomes significantly more remote, with mountains cut by deep river valleys and lochs. At the southern foothills of the Cairngorm Mountains stand Balmoral Castle, the winter retreat of the Royal Family every since Prince Albert purchased the entire estate for £31,000 in 1852. The quiet and gentle activities pursued here are quite different from those on the other side of the Cairngorms. Aviemore in the Spey Valley is a multi-million-pound holiday centre, open all year round. It resembles a mediterranean resort in summer and an

Alpine ski centre in the winter. Despite such commercialism it is quite possible for the visitor with a more exploratory nature to enjoy the same scenery but with space and tranquillity only a short walk away.

Of all the legends associated with this area, that of the Loch Ness monster is perhaps the most well-known. It has become almost institutionalized as a tourist attraction, and almost every year the mystery is fanned into life again by some new evidence or sighting. Nevertheless, there is something unfathomable about it, as reports of 'Nessie' go back to the 1870s, long before tourism, and many witnesses have been respectable people, and stone cold sober. The only thing to come up from Loch Ness recently, however, was the wreck of a Wellington Bomber, which crashed there during World War II.

Hundreds of years ago the northern islands were inhabited by the Vikings, and therefore it is not surprising to find that many visitors to Orkney and Shetland are Scandinavians who want to see the well-preserved remains of their ancestors' homes. Skara Brae is one such settlement. It was buried by driftsand, which effectively preserved the intricate complex of buildings as well as the stone furniture and the drainage system.

South of Cape Wrath is some of Britain's wildest and most barren country. Quartzite peaks glisten in the sun like glass mountains, and rough scree rises to heights of around 2500 feet. The west coast is a myriad of lochs, bays, peninsulas and islands. The most remote islands are the Outer Hebrides, most of which are reached by ferries from Ullapool, Oban and Mallaig. The village of Mallaig lies at the end of the renowned 'Road to the Isles'. This narrow winding track has featured many times in songs and films, as it passes through the most beautiful scenery. At its western end this road crosses a narrow ribbon of land separating Loch Morar from the sea. At 1017 feet in depth this is the deepest lake in Britain, and lies in the same region as the country's highest mountain, Ben Nevis, which rises to an incredible 4406 feet.

Scotland also boasts Britain's largest lake, Loch Lomond, the 'Queen of the Scottish lakes'. The familiar ballad of Loch Lomond is said to have been composed, on the eve of his execution, by a follower of Bonnie Prince Charlie. 'I'll take the low road' is taken to mean that his spirit will arrive in his native Scotland after his death sooner than his friend travelling by the more traditional means on the 'high road'. It is a poignant song which reflects sentiments held by many Scots, including those who now live in many different parts of the world. Scotland will always be their home.

But whatever road you take, the spirit of Scotland makes for a distinct and unforgettable visit.

Opposite: *The Ring of Brogar, one of Orkney's many ancient and mysterious sites.*
Above left: *Waulkmill Bay, Orkney.*
Left: *Looking across Kilbrannan Sound from Kintyre towards the Island of Arran.*
Overleaf: *An isolated cottage in the Scottish Highlands.*